Autism

The Autism Spectrum, Explained

From Autism Diagnosis to Autism Care

2nd Edition

Fred Cremone

information is without contract or any type of guarantee assurance.

The trademarks that are used are without any consent, and the publication of the trademark is without permission or backing by the trademark owner. All trademarks and brands within this book are for clarifying purposes only and are the owned by the owners themselves, not affiliated with this document.

TABLE OF CONTENTS

Introduction

Autism is a word that can send a shiver of fear through every parent of a young child. Questions quickly pop up in a parent's mind. What will this mean for my child's social interactions? Will they be able to be independent? How will they function in school? Will this diagnosis limit or disrupt their ability to learn? With all the misconceptions and misinformation about autism, parents are left with a sense of hopelessness, feeling that a diagnosis of autism is the end of their child's hopes and dreams. This disorder spectrum appears to limit their child's potential to achieve adult independence, because so much of the information available focuses on the negative.

But there is so much more to autism than the worst case scenarios touted in the media. Autism encompasses a large number of disorders, creating what is known as the autism spectrum. For the disorders within this spectrum, there are a number of treatments and therapies available. Autistic individuals can and do function in society, and in many cases these children can thrive in their future, being independent and successfully managing the effects of autism.

One critical component that determines what a child can achieve is their parents, both their involvement with therapy and positive reinforcement. The more involved the parents are, the better an outcome their children can have, regardless of where they fall in the spectrum. But parents find themselves in a situation where the stress, including emotional, physical and mental, can be extremely draining. So how can a family help their autistic child, while managing the stress such a diagnosis can entail?

Over the next few chapters, we are going to take an in-depth look at autism, starting with some historical background. Then we will explore what the autism spectrum means and what is involved in the diagnosis process. Of course, as with all other disorders that people aren't widely familiar with, autism suffers with its own myths. We'll take a moment to bust a few of those myths here, although it won't be all inclusive.

We'll also take time to discuss how parents can be a support system for their children. After all, the most important person your child has in their corner is you.

Focusing on a positive note, we'll talk about current therapies and what the future of autistic research looks like. In addition, this book takes a look at how early intervention can help a child grow to their full potential, as well as explore some potential pitfalls for teenagers and adults with autism. After all, they can't stay little forever. So let's get started by getting a little background on autism.

Chapter 1:
The Background of Autism

Autism is based on a Greek word "autos" meaning self. In 1908, a psychiatrist named Eugen Bleuler used the term autism to describe a schizophrenic patient that had withdrawn into his own little world. Bleuler defined it as a morbid self-admiration and self-withdrawal. These individuals he observed were often so withdrawn that they had limited or no social interactions with others.

Overtime, withdrawal continued to play a part in defining autism but through the observations of scientists and doctors, autism came to mean so much more. Today, we define autism based on development delays and other symptoms. Yet none of that would be possible without these early observations of children who stood out from the crowd.

Two of the first pioneers in autism research were Hans Asperger and Leo Kanner. In the 1940s, these two men were working separately on their research, but their observations remained useful to physicians for the next three decades. So what did these two men observe in their patients?

Kanner noted difficulties in social interactions, difficulty adapting to change, good memories, a sensitivity to stimuli (particularly sound), resistance or allergies to food, intellectual potential, a propensity to repeat words, and difficulty with spontaneous activity.

Asperger, the same scientist whom Asperger's Syndrome was named after, noticed similar symptoms as Kenner, although not necessarily the repeating words. Instead, Asperger noted that the children appeared to speak as grown-ups.

While these children struggled in several areas, they did appear to exhibit advanced intelligence capabilities, such as good memories and advanced speaking skills. Others tested higher on IQ tests. Yet their struggles in other areas remained.

Additionally, the children seemed very clumsy and different from other children in terms of their fine motor skills. Autism can impair gross motor skills due to neurological problems and sensory processing. Learning how to swim or ride a bike can be difficult because the child may have difficulty with body awareness, balance and motor control. The fine motor skill challenges that Asperger observed includes challenges with writing, drawing and getting dressed, probably due to a lack of motor control in the small muscles of the hands.

Since development depends on building these early skill sets, particularly language skills and more technical abilities, the lack of imitation ability or fine motor skills snowballs for these children, thus creating larger development gaps as they continue to grow.

Kenner and a scientist named Bruno Bettelheim defined the cause of autism with a hypothesis that the mothers of these children were cold toward them, implying the root of the problem was parenting skills. The social and mental withdrawal by these children was attributed to a lack of love expressed by the parents, particularly the mothers. But not everyone in the scientific and psychological community agreed with this hypothesis.

One such dissenter was psychologist Bernard Rimland, whose son was diagnosed with autism. In 1964, Rimland published a book called *Infantile Autism: The Syndrome and its Implications for a Neural Theory of Behavior*, discussing autism and proposing that it was due to a neurological cause, not due to parenting skills. His voice and research challenged Bettelheim's frigid mother theory, resulting in some of the first support groups for parents of these unique children.

However, this initial theory continues to persist in society's consciousness, in large part because of the lack of understanding about how autism can present. A parent taking an autistic child out may have to deal with behaviors that most people would view as a temper tantrum or fit. Thus, people reinforce their own misperceptions regarding these spectrum disorders.

Throughout the 1970s and 1980s, psychologists and the scientific community's understanding of autism grew, although it was still being grouped with mental retardation and psychosis. Foundations and other groups, including The Erica Foundation, began using education and therapy to treat autism, but these therapies were based on psychosis treatments. Although Asperger had been occupied with creating a body of research and observations, it wasn't until the 1980s that his work was translated into English and joined the growing body of research on autism.

Potential neurological disturbances research started in earnest during the 1980s. It was during this time that autism was finally separated from mental retardation and psychosis. Researchers looked at a variety of neurological causes and other genetic ailments they felt could be at the core of autism. Other researchers continued to add the body of knowledge regarding autism and the development of the spectrum, particularly because they were defining the symptoms that autistic children consistently had. This included observing and recording inconsistent behaviors and development delays. As a result, there was a growing body of knowledge that allowed for a clinical definition of autism. Still, there is no definitive blood test or lab that can be done to confirm autism. In this area, research is still ongoing.

Notable ones included Lorna Wing and Christopher Gillberg, Swedish researchers who founded the Wing's triad, which included disturbed mutual contact, disturbed mutual communication and limited imagination. During the 1990s, they added another factor, limited planning ability, turning the triad into a square. Additionally, Ole Ivar Lovaas furthered behavioral analysis and treatment of autism. His behavior therapy targeted younger children (those less than 5 years old) with intensive therapy, both in the office and at home.

It is this research that provided the basis for today's early intervention therapies. Today, many researchers have compiled data that supports a defined window of opportunity with the best results. Earlier intervention, before the age of two, has been demonstrated to provide the best outcomes. Yet with a standard diagnosis age of 5, that window is often closed or almost so. Results of therapy can then be mixed.

For parents, this can be particularly frustrating, because an autism diagnosis can only be made with a compilation of data confirming developmental delay, which takes time. Research to a genetic or lab test continues in the hopes of catching these children earlier and beginning intervention sooner.

As research continues, behavior therapy continues to be one of the main focuses for those with autism, along with prescription drug therapies. But before we discuss therapies, it's important to define autism based on the scientific community's current understanding and what they use to clinically define autism.

What is Autism?

Autism is not a single disease, but actually describes a range of developmental disorders, known as autistic spectrum disorders (ASD). Typically, these disorders are diagnosed in childhood and will carry on into adulthood. ASD has a wide variety of manifestations, which can be categorized into three broad groups.

1. Problems with social interactions – Affected children may have difficulty appreciating the emotions and feelings of others.

2. Problems with language and communication skills – This manifests as delayed language development and often a difficulty in starting conversations.

3. Unusual behaviors and patterns of thoughts – Typically, this includes repetitive movements and activities, or the child may often get upset if routines are altered in any significant way.

The frequency of autism diagnosis is on the rise. In England, for example, there is an estimated 1 in 100 kids with ASD. According to the Centers for Disease Control and Prevention (CDC), autism occur regardless of racial, ethnic and socioeconomic groups, although it appears to be five times more common in boys than girls. The CDC estimates 1 in 88 children are diagnosed with ASD, but those number do fluctuate as the clinical definition continues to be refined.

Over the last two decades, the number of autism cases appears to be on the rise. Some experts argue that this rise may be due in part to health professionals being better educated and able to diagnosis cases correctly. Before this better understanding of autism, children with autism would be missed or labelled as "painfully shy" or "slow", but there was no options given to those parents, who could tell that it was more than simply a case shy behavior.

Because autism falls on a spectrum, it includes a variety of levels of severity. For parents, this can mean having a high functioning autistic child or one that may need more intense assistance. Some types of ASD include:

- Autistic disorder, otherwise referred to as "classic autism" – This disorder manifests with substantial language delays, social and speech issues, as well as unusual behaviors. Other additional disabilities may occur, but this is not always the case.

- Asperger syndrome – These symptoms are milder than classic autism, but include social delays and unusual behaviors. Typically, there are no language problems or intellectual disability.

- Pervasive developmental disorder, known as "atypical autism" – These are the disorders not otherwise specified (PDD-NOS). These individuals display criteria for autistic disorder or Asperger syndrome, but not all the criteria. Their symptoms may be fewer and milder, but the fundamental social and speech issues are still present.

While not specifically labeled as autism, those with ASD may also have other difficulties, such as attention deficit hyperactivity disorder (ADHD), Tourette's syndrome or other tic disorders and dyspraxia (developmental co-ordination disorder), although this is not a comprehensive list.

These other difficulties can often make the autism worse or contribute to the children feeling more isolated. Parents need to be aware of these accompanying difficulties and how they can make things more difficult for their children. The treatments may result in having to combine treatments, both behavioral and pharmaceutical, so it's important that all of your child's medical team is aware of what they have been prescribed and are currently taking. This will help to avoid adverse reactions and potential negative side effects.

Those with mild to moderate disorders classified as ASD, but who have average or above-average intelligence, can grow to be independent adults with families and long term relationships. Yet those individuals who may have below-intelligence concerns may find it difficult to live independently, requiring them to have additional care and assistance throughout their lives. Parents may find themselves as caregivers long past the time when children traditionally leave home. Combined with aging parents and their own health concerns, the families of children with autism may struggle to care for everyone's needs, emotionally, physically and mentally.

Families therefore find autism is a disorder that has long term implications and can be a scary diagnosis when first received. Parents ask themselves, what will be the future for my child? How affective will the therapies be? As we explore autism further, we will see how the future is bright for children with autism and the research is trying to brighten that light every day.

In defining autism, the spectrum has been referred to several times. So what is the autism spectrum and how do the doctors diagnose some with ASD?

Chapter 2:
Learning about the Autism Spectrum and Diagnosis

Autism is part of has been defined as five pervasive developmental disorders (PDD). These are characterized by:

- deviations of social interactions and communication

- restricted interests

- highly repetitive behavior

Autism itself has a wide range of severity with a large variety of symptoms. All the disorders that fall within the spectrum have their own unique characteristics. Additionally, just because you have one disorder, does not guarantee that you will have all of them. For example, individuals with a diagnosis of Asperger syndrome typically have no substantial delay in their language development. Autism can also be defined by low muscle tone and seizures. They might suffer from anxiety and also struggle with any change to their routine.

Autism itself may be referred to by such names as autistic disorder, childhood autism or infantile autism. For some individuals autism may be manifest in their silence or evident only as a mental disability. In other children, there could be repetitive movements, which could include hand flapping and rocking.

Some autistic individuals may be normal in most areas of life except for their social awkwardness. These children may have narrowly focused interests, and wordy, pedantic communication. Boundaries within ASD categories are necessarily arbitrary because of the overlapping symptoms and the myriad of features.

Throughout the diagnosis process, doctors and medical staff are observing and documenting various behaviors, developmental delays and other medical struggles that a child may have. By combining all this information, they can see not only where the child will land on the spectrum, but what other disorders or supplemental difficulties, such as ADD, may contribute to the child's delays. This information will also help them to draft the best intervention plan for a child, based on their unique needs.

Another important thing to remember is that social withdrawal may define autism but does not mean that these children prefer isolation. Yet making and maintaining friendships often proves to be very difficult for those individuals because of the delays in picking up or understanding non-spoken social cues. For these children, gaining and maintaining quality friendships is more important predictor of how lonely they are, not necessarily the number of their friends.

Autism can be diagnosed in children at around two years old. However, a diagnosis is easier to confirm as the child gets older and the development delays become more pronounced. Today, adults are being diagnosed with ASD that were missed in childhood. Since there isn't blood test to determine autism, doctors rely on behavioral, speech and movement observations to diagnosis a child, doctors have developed various screening tools to help them access whether a child is falls within the autism spectrum.

Developmental screening are short tests to define if a child is picking up basic skills when they should, or if they might be facing delays. During developmental screening, the pediatrician questions a parent about how their child is doing at hitting various milestones. Another option is for the physician to talk and play with the child, while observing their behavior and reactions to various stimulation. Any noticeable delay in these areas such as behavior, speech or movement could be a sign of a potential problem. If a problem is noticed, the doctor may recommend additional testing and even an appointment with a specialist to determine what may be causing the delay. Not all delays are necessarily caused by autism, but it also needs to be ruled out.

These developmental types of screenings typically occur at wellness or well child doctor visits. These visits occur at 9, 18, 24 and 30 months. A child born prematurely or with a low birth weight may need additional monitoring and developmental screening as they mature. It is important to discuss your child's behavior with your doctor and let them know if you notice any of these types of developmental delays, such as speech or lack of social interaction with siblings, parents or other caregivers.

In addition, all children ought to be vetted specifically for ASD during regular well-child doctor visits at 18 and 24 months. This is the time period that has been identified as most critical for therapeutic intervention. Research has found that therapeutic intercession at this young age can have a positive outcome in reducing the impact of these delays on their social interactions. Additional analysis might also be required if a child is considered at high risk for ASD. Some factors putting a child at high risk include having a sister, brother or other family with a diagnosis with ASD, or if ASD behaviors are existing in the child's development.

The importance of development delay screening for children can't be underestimated, but it's especially critical to monitor those who have greater risk factors for developmental problems due to preterm birth, low birth weight, or having a sibling with an ASD.

Understanding the Developmental Milestones

During their first year of life, babies are learning many new skills that help them explore the world around them. These busy bees are acquire the ability to focus their vision, reach out, explore, and accumulate knowledge about the world that they are growing up in.

Cognitive development involves the learning process of memory, language, thinking and reasoning. Learning language is more than just making various sounds or vocalizing "ma-ma" and "da-da". Listening, making connections between objects and the words that describe them, and understanding the names of people and things are all a part of the ongoing process of language development.

This is also a critical junction for your child's emotional growth. At this time in their lives, babies develop bonds of trust and love with not only their parents, but also extended family and friends. This is part of their emotional and social development, which is a key area for possible signs of autism. Parents are the first model of affection for their babies. The way they cuddle, hold, and play with them, sets the basis for their interactions with others, including their parents.

The next few years will see your child moving to make eye contact, talk with others and move from playing by themselves to playing with others, eventually interacting through group games. While it is not uncommon for children to develop a skill and then lose it while focusing on another, this is typically temporary.

Let your pediatrician know if skills are lost and don't appear to be returning or if more skills are disappearing. This is a regressive state and may be a sign of autism or another developmental delay. It cannot be stressed enough how important it is to utilize early detection methods to help your child. As we will see later on, the early detection of autism can lead to early intervention, which can be critical to how much progress your child can make learning skills and reversing their developmental delays, among other things.

When a development delay is not treated early on, the child can suffer in many ways. One of the most apparent is the frustration they may feel at school, as they can't make progress that matches their peers. After a while, they will lose interest in school. Even if these children get assistance later, it may be too late to reengage them into the educational process.

Additionally, a child suffers from emotional setbacks. They find themselves isolated from their peers. For the child that is different, they may find themselves the target of teasing, bullying and other negative behaviors. These will take an emotional toll over time. As we will learn, autistic children are more vulnerable to other mental disorders, particularly depression. When they struggle with emotional anxiety, it can lead to an increased likelihood of depression. That same anxiety can only increase their disorder's challenges, meaning that they can fall even further behind due to the emotional and physical stress. What happens when they lose precious learning time as younger children?

With a lack of a solid education under their belt, they may find it hard to remain independent as adults or reach their full potential. Every parent longs for their children to reach their potential, so it's important to pay attention to their overall development, particularly at these early stages of growth. If you see any signs for concern, it's important to bring it immediately to your doctor's attention. As a parent of a potentially autistic child, you are their voice and advocate. So what does the doctor look for that triggers an autistic diagnosis versus simply a small developmental setback?

Development: What Your Doctor Looks For

If your pediatrician is not checking your child with a type of ASD developmental screening test, as your child's advocate, ask that this screening test be done. Having these screening tests done is especially important if you have notices signs of delay in speech, a lack of fine motor skills or that your child is socially withdrawn from their siblings or others. Remember the signs of social withdrawal will be more pronounced than a child who might initially be shy around new people.

If the doctor perceives any signs of a problem, a complete investigative assessment is needed. This in-depth review involves detailed analysis of a child's behavior and development. Other aspects of this screening may include hearing and vision tests, genetic testing, neurological testing and additional medical tests as your doctor may see fit.

In some cases, your pediatrician might refer the child and family to a specialist for more assessment and comprehensive diagnosis. Specialists that provide these specialized assessments include:

- Developmental Pediatricians – Doctors are trained in child development and working with children with distinctive needs.

- Child Neurologists – These doctors concentrate on the brain, spine and nerves.

- Child Psychologists or Psychiatrists – Doctors are trained to understand how the human mind functions and provide therapy or behavioral training.

These specialists are trained not only in diagnosing autism spectrum disorder, but they play a part in helping to develop the best therapy program for an autistic child. While autism does have specifically defined clinical symptoms, each child can vary in what symptoms and delays they present. As a result, therapy and treatment have become very individualized.

While the way parents raise their children isn't a source of autism (see Chapter 3 on Autism Myth Busters), their genetics may contribute to an increased risk of having a child with autism. How so?

Genetics Play a Part

Autism can also be divided into syndromic and non-syndromic. Often associated with severe or profound retardation, syndromic autism is also marked by congenital features, including tuberous sclerosis. Genetic studies have shown that individuals with various genetic disorders, including Fragile X syndrome, may be more likely to have ASD in conjunction with them.

Autism may also be a regressive type. In these children, the diagnosis of autism is made on the basis lack of language or social skills, as opposed to a lack of forward progress, typically during the period of 15 to 30 months of age. This could be considered a specific subtype of autism.

It is important to note that these children can make social connections, but they don't necessarily make those deep connections with their caregivers. For example, three to five year old autistic children are less able to exhibit social understanding, go up to others spontaneously, imitate and respond to emotions, connect nonverbally, and taking turns with others. Apart from diagnosis of individual subtypes through interview based tests, there are other tests that can be useful. Research into a variety of areas, such as fMRI, can help identify biologically relevant subtypes of this gene which can be identified using brain scans. This information can aid further neuro-genetic studies of autism.

Genetic research is also being pursued to define the autism subtypes. For example, Type 1 autism characterizes very rare autism cases where a mutation in their CNTNAP2 gene has been detected. Through these types of tests, an autism diagnosis can be made. While none of these tests have yet come to the mainstream and defining developmental delays is still the primary diagnostic tool, these tests give hope to parents that early diagnosis will be possible. With early diagnosis comes early intervention, which is so critical for autistic children.

At that point of diagnosis, the doctor will work extensively with you and your family to come up with a treatment plan that will help your child manage and even excel with their diagnosis. But as with most disorders and diseases, treatment plans can be altered if various therapies are not having the desired effect.

But before we talk about various treatment options available, let's bust a few of the myths about the autism spectrum disorders.

Chapter 3:
Autism Myth Busters

Individuals with autism may have differences that result in social, speech and other challenges, but this does not mean that they can't or don't make connections with others. It can be difficult at times to understand how they process social interactions, but below are a few myths about autism and the myth-busting truths.

Myth #1 – They don't want friends.

People with autism don't want friends, but the reality is that these children or individuals struggle with social skills, making it difficult for them to build friendships. While they might appear shy or unfriendly, it's just their incapability to communicate and understand basic social cues. Autism effects the ability of the individual to understand unspoken social cues, such as sarcasm or body language, but they do understand emotions themselves. When it comes to more direct social cues, they can better understand these and act on them. ASD children can feel empathy and compassion, even if they lack the social cues to express it in a way others will understand.

Myth #2 – They don't express or feel emotions.

Autistic individuals can't feel or express any emotions, but the truth is autistic individuals express their emotions differently, due to their inability to process social cues. They will also process your emotions and expressions differently, because they might not be able to understand your social cues.

Imagine being blind and not having the ability to see a person's expression. That challenge can make it difficult to gauge social cues. While an individual who is blind can still do extremely well socially, it takes time and a bit of a learning curve for them to translate social cues in a new way. An autistic child, while not visually challenged, is technically in the same boat. They can't process social cues in the same way others do. As a result, they need to be taught how to do so. It doesn't mean that they can't or they won't have the ability, but it will take time to learn and make part of their everyday behavior. Even those who have used therapy successfully, may find that they analyze situations where most of us act instinctively.

Myth #3 – They are struggling intellectually.

Autism means intellectually disabled, but in truth autism also brings wonderful abilities, including high IQs. Some individuals excel at math, music or other areas. While some autistic individuals may have some mental disabilities, this is not universal. Characteristics of autism will vary from person to person.

Often, autism blesses those diagnosed with an analytical and extremely orderly way of looking at things. This means that these children who might struggle with language, can find success in the sciences. An autistic child may have developmental delays, but it shouldn't reflect on their intellectual abilities. In fact, from an intellectual perspective, these children may find a place to truly shine.

Myth #4 – It's all in their heads.

Autism is just a brain disorder, but the reality is that individuals can also suffer from gastro-intestinal disorders, food sensitivities, and a variety of allergies. Autistic children may display other physical and mental issues in addition to their ASD. These can range from depression to excessive alcohol use, or related health issues. Even unrelated health issues may be enhanced by the autism.

So parents find themselves not just dealing with a child's behavior issues or developmental delays, but also additional health concerns. As a result, they may find themselves coordinating medical treatments across several different disciplines.

Myth #5 – Parenting or lack of it is to blame.

Autism is a product of poor parenting or a lack of parenting skills. While this was the prevailing hypothesis in the 1950s, researchers have since proved that this is not the case. Parenting skills do not give an individual autism, since this is a neurological spectrum disorder. Time and again, parenting has been proven to not be the cause, yet when a child is acting out in public, society still deems it to be the lack of good parenting. Societal prejudices and assumptions continue to give this myth life. But how do these prejudices and judgements take root? Part of the struggle for autistic families is that what people can see and associate with is the outward behavior, versus what they can't, the internal workings of their child's brain. Often times the inability to see the underlying causes of a behavior can result in judgements and prejudices being reinforced instead of being broken down.

Myth #6 – Autism diagnosis is on the rise.

The prevalence of autism has dramatically increased. Within the last 40 years, the definition of autism has been refined for doctors and physicians, so more individuals are being properly diagnosed. The addition of better diagnostic tools have given doctors the ability to find and intervene earlier for an autistic patient.

Myth #7 – Autism is covered by all insurance plans, including federal ones, in all states.

Autism therapies are covered by insurance, but the reality is that most insurance companies exclude ASD from their coverage plans. Only 25 states in the U.S. require insurance companies to cover treatments for ASD, although the fight to make it all 50 states continues.

Additionally, what is covered as part of ASD treatment can vary from insurance plan to Medicaid. Families in one state may carry a larger financial burden than others just across the state line. As a result, many families struggle with the financial burden of providing necessary treatments, behavioral interventions and other medical care.

As you can see, these myths are varied but they all survive due to a lack of information about autism in the public consciousness. Today, many families and organizations are working hard to change society's perceptions of this disorder spectrum. Their work will ultimately allow for the children and adults with these disorders to live in a society that is more accepting of their differences. Parents of autistic children long for a day when their children are not only accepted but celebrated for their unique perspectives.

Another source of debate in the world of autism doesn't revolve around a myth, but instead the misinformation about something your child receives at their pediatrician's during their wellness visits.

The Debate: To Vaccinate or Not?

Other misinformation about autism relates to intense debates about what causes autism. One of the biggest debates revolves around vaccines. Initial studies by certain scientists seemed to indicate that there was a link between vaccines and autism. Hundreds of individuals stopped vaccinating their children, not willing to risk their children developing an autistic disorder. These parents reasoned that the risk of developing the diseases these vaccines prevent was less than the risk of autism. Thus, they made the call not to vaccinate, relying on others to vaccinate and thus protect their children via herd immunity. The problem was that the reduction of vaccinated children reduced the protection of herd immunity, impart because the vaccinated herd was much smaller.

In fact, a recent study published in the journal Pediatrics showed that one in four parents is concerned that vaccines can cause autism. So what started this debate?

In the late 1990s, Andrew Wakefield, M.D. published a paper in the Lancet, a professional medical journal, which suggested the MMR vaccine for mumps, measles and rubella might cause autism like symptoms in children.

According to Paul Offit, chief of infectious diseases at the Children's Hospital in Philadelphia, Wakefield did a case study with eight children as his subjects. These children had received the MMR vaccine, then later developed signs of autism. Wakefield also noted his subjects had abnormalities in their intestinal tracts, including inflammation. As a result of his case study, Wakefield proposed a new syndrome that linked this intestinal inflammation to the MMR and that this inflammation caused autism symptoms. Hence, he believed that the vaccine was a link between autism and a potential cause of the autism spectrum disorder.

Though Wakefield did acknowledge that he couldn't definitively link the MMR with autism, he did work for a well-respected hospital in England and his paper was being published by an impressive medical journal. This gave his study credit and weight that it might not have otherwise received. The result was that many people skipped over the lack of a definitive connection and instead took his theory and turned it into fact. Within the scientific community, this hypothesis came under fire, but without any research to refute it, parents were quickly confused about whether vaccines were the best choice for their children.

In England, for example, thousands of parents refused vaccines for their children. This resulted in spikes of medical conditions that hadn't been around in years, as children were hospitalized for measles, with three deaths in Ireland alone. The spark started by this small study meant that vaccines were reworked and new studies were launched to attempt to understand if there was indeed a connection. Those vaccines that were formulated to allow for multiple doses were redone to make them single use vaccines, as well as separating some of these vaccines back into single versus combo vaccines. Those vaccines being sold as single doses means that in other countries, vaccinations have increased in price because they only can get one dose per vial instead of several doses in that same vial.

Thus the debate over vaccines and autism has spilled over into less developed countries, where diseases such as measles are a real and potentially deadly concern. By making vaccines more expensive, these individuals may struggle to vaccinate their families against diseases that may not be in the U.S. but are still real threats in other parts of the world.

Stop for a minute and imagine how much weight those against vaccines must have been able to execute to facilitate changes of this magnitude, without any scientific evidence to back their claims that these vaccines and their ingredients contributed to autism. Yet, their voices were so loud that vaccines were reworked to address their concerns, at a cost of millions of dollars.

Yet another of the main reasons why anyone talks about vaccines and autism is that a few parents noticed changes in their children, within a short period of time after being vaccinated. Their children appeared to be developing normally, then their development seems to suddenly stop, particularly in their lack of social interactions with family and friends, as well as lost language abilities. This has been called regressive autism, which is a source of controversy because major researchers in autism believe the disorders are always present versus taking away development.

They argue that the parents just didn't notice the delays because the child was younger and they weren't as evident. Most delays become more apparent as a child becomes more active, but can be less evident in young babies, particularly those around the 2-6 months age range.

Most medical researchers argue that the appearance of regressive development is probably a coincidence, because the period when autism will become most apparent due to development delays is during the timeframe when routine vaccines are also scheduled. For example, parents may not initially notice delayed development in eye fixation in their child at 2 months, but other symptoms, in combination with the lack of eye fixation, which are used to diagnose autism, may become more apparent around the time of initial or second round vaccinations.

Although there are two distinct issues concerning vaccines and autism, these issues often get lumped together. One concern has to do with the measles, mumps and rubella (MMR) vaccine; the other involves vaccines containing the thimerosal, which contains a form of mercury suspected of causing autism.

Thimerosal is a chemical preservative that has recently been removed from most vaccines it was used in, due in part to concerns from various advocacy groups who saw it as a risk. There is no evidence that thimerosal actually contributes to autism, but there is also not enough evidence to definitively refute this connection. As a result, it has been removed, thus quietly silencing the controversy in this aspect of the great vaccine debates.

Yet it is that lack of publicity that gives those against vaccinations such power. They are vocal and using social media to further their cause. The scientific knowledge available about autism or the lack of a connection between vaccines and autism is lost under the more dramatic stories from parents that have continued to go viral.

Societies and foundations working toward a better understanding of autism struggle to make sure the most current scientific information is available to their parents and members. While vaccines can cause various reactions, these tend to be more allergic in nature. While it can feel safe to blame vaccines and choose not to vaccinate, parents are leaving their children at risk for diseases that are now on the move across the globe thanks to prevalence of international travel.

What the Research Shows

Throughout a period of 15 years after Wakefield published his study, at least eighteen controlled studies have scrutinized a potential link between autism spectrum disorders (ASD) and vaccines. All this research has resulted in a large database of medical evidence demonstrating no link of vaccines being a source or cause of autism.

Those studies took up two primary theories: Wakefield's hypothesis that the MMR vaccine was linked to autism and a potential cause of the disorder. The other theory stated thimerosal, a preservative with mercury in it, was the guilty party.

In a 2004 report analyzing the research into the possible connections, the Institute of Medicine, a national public health organization, concluded that the body of evidence favors rejection of a causal relationship between autism and both the MMR vaccine and thimerosal.

That same year, 10 of the 13 authors of the Wakefield study retracted it, listing various flaws in the study. These scientists were willing to admit that the study drew erroneous conclusions regarding autism and vaccines. In February 2010, The Lancet retracted Wakefield's entire study after an independent government review concluded that he had acted "dishonestly and irresponsibly" in conducting his research.

This dishonest and unethical behavior included undertaking unnecessary and painful procedures on the children in his study. Wakefield also did not disclose the fact that he had been a paid consultant to two attorneys. What made this worse is that these attorneys were representing parents who believed their children had been harmed by the MMR vaccine. These parents were suing and of course, Wakefield's research was part of their arsenal. In the spring of 2010, Wakefield lost his license to practice medicine in the U.K. While he continues to deny any wrongdoing, Wakefield has been ostracized within the scientific community.

Yet in spite of the discipline Wakefield received from the scientific community and his own team being willing to retract their work, the public continues to believe that a connection between autism and vaccines as a potential cause still exists. The increased understanding of autism has led to a greater number of diagnosed individuals, so what was once a sideline disorder is now much more prevalent in the public eye.

Today, it is more common than ever for parents to know an autistic child or to know an individual related to someone with autism. Those same parents are unlikely to know or have known anyone who suffered or even died from smallpox or the measles. Vaccines were created to prevent these diseases and many others. Today, there are numerous vaccines for a variety of diseases, including chickenpox. More vaccines continue to be developed, and so parents are presented with a large amount of information and struggle to decide what they want to vaccinate their children against. The CDC has made a list of what it deems to be necessary vaccinations, or its standard list. Advocacy groups argue that parents have the right to refuse certain vaccines, even the ones on the list, without medical cause. These exemptions have come under fire, because the more that take advantage of them, the greater the risk to overall herd immunity.

While the debate continues over exemptions and whether they should be allowed for personal or religious reasons, parents are still trying to make the best choices for their families in a sea of conflicting information.

With the scare from the Wakefield study and continual sharing of stories from family members of autistic children claiming a connection does exist using social media as their platform, parents find themselves at a loss to define the true risk versus reward ratio of vaccines.

Notable figures, including actress Jenny McCarthy, an autism advocate who believes her son's autism may have been caused by vaccines, also lend reliability to the idea that there is a link between the two. When the outbreak of measles occurred in 2014, starting at Disney Land, those who had chosen not to vaccinate were vilified for what individuals felt was their contribution to the spread of the disease.

Herd immunization was explained in great detail, but for many of those who had chosen not to vaccinate, the arguments did not deter them. In fact, many strengthen their resolve, even as their children were quarantined and many denied access to school until they had passed the incubation period for measles. The debate about vaccines has grown into a larger discussion about the rights of individuals versus the rights of society as a whole. At what point can the government make medical decisions for the individual? By making vaccines legally mandatory, individuals argue that the government is stepping over its bounds and into the individual's right to choose the medical inventions they will accept.

While some children may have adverse reactions to vaccines, including allergies that prevent them from being vaccinated, a vast majority of children do not have this issue. The children who do have allergies are also depending on the herd immunity affect, because they do not have the same ability to build an immunity via vaccine that those who have been vaccinated do. Yet these children and their families find themselves tarred with the anti-vaccine crowd. Many have spoken out to discuss how their families also must deal with the quarantines, despite their support for vaccines. Those who can vaccine group these children with medical exemptions in the same group, which can make these families feel isolated in a much larger debate.

For the parents who choose not to vaccinate, avoiding anything that they appears to be a risk leading to autism can seem safer than choosing to get a vaccine for diseases that seem unlikely to occur.

A report from the Centers for Disease Control and Prevention (CDC) concludes that a 2008 measles outbreak in San Diego, yet another example of how the herd immunity is being eroded, triggered by an unvaccinated child who traveled from Europe, struck people who had purposely not been vaccinated against the disease. These outbreaks will continue to disproportionately affect those who are not vaccinated, due to the overall reduction of the herd immunity in their communities.

Amy Pisani, the executive director of Every Child by Two which advocates for childhood immunization, recognizes the indecision parents have when they enter their pediatrician's office. Her organization, originally founded to train nurses and help low-income parents access government run free vaccination programs, now spends 70 percent of its time addressing parental safety concerns about vaccines and the importance of sticking to your child's vaccination schedule. Every Child By Two has since created a website and dedicated themselves to educating parents with medically sound data before they make a decision to vaccinate or not.

The need for research continues because until a definitive cause for autism is found, it will be hard to completely rid people of the notion there is a connection between vaccines and autism. In the meantime, each family has to take the medical knowledge currently available and make an informed decision for their children. Research is continually ongoing in an attempt to find the cause of autism, but while a cause has not yet been found, effective therapies to manage the disorder have been discovered.

Chapter 4:
Current Therapies

It is clear there is much more to learn about autism spectrum disorder (ASD), especially in comparison to other disorders and diseases. For example, in December 2013, 131 clinical trials investigating autism were currently recruiting on www.clinicaltrials.gov, compared to a larger number of studies for other diseases and conditions. For example, there are up to 604 trials investigating asthma and more than 10,000 trials researching cancer.

The need for proven treatments prods many parents to follow their own research, using the trial and error option. A preliminary study conducted in 2004 found over a hundred different treatments being tried by families with an autistic child across the United States. The study also discovered, on average, parents were using up to seven different treatments at any one time. The number and types of treatments used varied according to the child's age and the severity of their disorder's symptoms. But many of these treatments lack empirical support to move them into the proven method column within the scientific community.

It can be overwhelming for families to navigate this large mountain of material. Although many start with the drive and determination to find the best individual treatment or treatment combination for their child, it can quickly avalanche, discouraging parents. On top of that, they are still parents, often with other children to care for, plus jobs and homes. Autism treatments can be expensive and time consuming, adding more strain to parents who might already feel on the edge.

Just Google autism treatments and a deluge of treatments fills your search results. The treatments promoted are as vast as the autism spectrum itself, ranging from the commonly accepted standards to the exotic and perhaps dangerous. While some options offer reasonable solutions, others promise a cure and/or complete recovery from ASD but only if you are willing to pull out the proverbial checkbook. For families struggling with autism, some of those exotic cures may provide false hope, but a hope they are still willing to grab for.

For service providers and other professionals in the field, the landscape of ASD treatments and therapies is just as frustrating. The diverse nature of the disorder makes it challenging to diagnose and treat as well as create effective research plans. In response to this challenge, researchers are now identifying children on the spectrum with similar characteristics, creating autism subtypes, which can be easier to study. By using autism subtypes, it is hoped that treatment studies can be better targeted to certain symptoms and thus be more likely to yield positive and definitive results.

Treatment plans have taken on a unique quality, truly reflective of the child and their specific needs. While this can helpful for one child, it makes finding over arcing treatments that can be used in clinical trials difficult and challenging to identify on a consistent basis.

Throughout history, there has been a path from folk cure to a proven medical treatment. On the other hand, there have been medical interventions, believed in for centuries, which were later proven to be ineffective and even fatal. Distinguishing quality and effective therapies from those based on theories and shoddy medical research is the result of carefully defined and well carried out scientific studies by qualified scientists and researchers.

Medical bodies of evidence are created through many forms of research. Methods range from an in-depth analysis of a single case, known as a case study, to the use of surveys and statistics to draw conclusions. Additionally, researchers use interviews to gather information on attitudes, beliefs, and behaviors of groups to large clinical trials testing the efficacy of new drugs or therapies. All have worth and contribute to the growing knowledge of autism.

Ideally, therapies and treatments for ASDs should be tested using a Randomized Controlled Trial (RCT), allowing any new therapy or treatment to be accepted as a standard within the scientific community. This method of research eliminates as much bias as possible, making the results value added to doctors and scientists. Valid treatments are legitimized and made available to those individuals who can benefit. Ineffective or dangerous treatments are debunked, protecting children and adults alike.

Educational and behavioral methods are often a core piece of an ASD treatment road map. There are many approaches currently being used, and new ones are being medically endorsed on a steady basis. Many of these interventions contrast not just in their application, but also in their philosophical slant to treating children with ASD. This is truly a spectrum disorder that is focused on creating a treatment plan that works for each child. Tailoring is an essential part of autism therapy and contributes to how research is conducted.

Limited evidence-based research is existing for most of the behavioral and/or educational based plans. These methods are particularly difficult to study using traditional research options. For one thing, a classroom or therapist's office isn't a laboratory setting with all of its filters to account for a variety of variables. Thus researchers find it difficult to control for the numerous factors that can obstruct or bias research results. Another difficulty is exactly reproducing any single intervention across multiple settings. Still, researchers continue to move forward with therapies that appear to consistently provide improvement for those who are able to take advantage of them in the pivotal period of autism.

Early Invention: An Effective Therapy

One bright spot is the mounting evidence supporting the use of early intensive intervention programs for children with ASD. Such programs generally involve hours of therapy every week, and appear to be most effective when done for children between the ages of 2 and 7.

As science continues to search for solutions, parents try what is available. There are some standard approaches put in place for almost every child, while there are other treatments that come and go in popularity. The top five interventions currently being used in the United States for children with ASD include Speech Therapy, Visual Schedules, Applied Behavioral Analysis (ABA), Social Stories and the Picture Exchange Communication System (PECS).

All of these interventions are used by more than one-quarter of families with children with ASD. Other popular behavioral and educational approaches include Cognitive/Behavioral Therapy, Discrete Trial Training (including Lovaas Therapy), Music therapy, Treatment and Education of Autistic and Related Communication-Handicapped Children (TEACCH), Floortime, and Augmentative and Alternative Communication Systems.

Early intensive intervention can change the outcome for young children with ASD. Two major academic approaches dominate the early intervention scene: a behavioral method and a developmental, relationship-based approach.

Applied Behavior Analysis (ABA) is one of the more well-known of the behavioral methods. Such programs focus on inspiring or reinforcing constructive behaviors while discouraging undesirable ones. Practitioners cautiously evaluate whether a child has been rewarded for any undesirable behaviors, and then ensure that this no longer happens. They then work to establish new behaviors using a variety of methods, including discrete trial training. For example, the child is directed to hand someone a pencil. If she does, then she receives a reward. If she doesn't, the reward is withheld, but a prompt is given to encourage the desired behavior. One such prompt may be gesturing toward the pencil.

Many studies have consistently shown that ABA and similar behavioral interventions can improve intelligence test scores, language skills, and academic performance of younger children with autism. Some studies have also shown some improvement in behavior or personal and social skills, while others have not. One issue has been generalization. It can be difficult to find evidence that shows children are transferring the skills they learned in one setting through the behavioral interventions to settings outside the one where the skills were gained.

Many children taking part in these programs do make substantial strides. Yet, such interventions have been found to lack results in a great number of affected children achieving normal developmental status, as it was initially thought. Instead, they achieve the ability to function better in society, but without very early intervention, the effects can be limited.

For children who have a limited result, they may find themselves on the opposite end of independence as an adult.

Developmental interventions take a different tack. The most well-known of these is Dr. Stanley Greenspan's Developmental, Individual-Difference, Relationship Based (DIR) model, of which Floortime is a major part.

Development refers to the manner of acquiring skills in different stages, from simpler to more complex. In Greenspan's view, the area of development where children with ASDs are most impacted is the ones involving higher order thinking and relating. This includes shared attention, to back and forth interactions, problem solving, all the way to abstract thought. Floortime is used to move a child up this developmental ladder using play. An adult follows the child's lead to engage in playtime, to create opportunities for connection, and therefore, build to more complex emotional and social relating. For instance, a child may be lining up trains, so the adult will get on the floor and do the same activity, trying to catch the child's interest and their glance, sharing any pleasure or frustration they may demonstrate.

Unfortunately, there is little evidence to prove this developmental approach is effective at present. According to the American Academy of Pediatrics, preliminary data is promising in showing overall improvement. However, additional studies will be needed to understand this model more fully.

Although the behavioral and developmental viewpoints are far apart, in theoretical terms, there is also overlap between various models. For example, naturalistic behavioral approaches are more child-centered, and Pivotal Response Training is behaviorally based, attempting to address core issues, such as the motivation to relate socially. As in developmental approaches, the hope is that improvements in this core area will translate into improvements in many other areas.

Over time, many programs have developed to include the best of both worlds: the intensive, behavioral focus of the ABA model and along with the relationship-rich, child-led focus of the Greenspan model.

Beyond the specific nature of any one approach, there are many other aspects that influence the outcomes of early intervention programs, such as location (think home-based vs. center-based), the duration and intensity of the therapy, the provider's experience and of course, parental involvement. In addition, characteristics of the child, such as age, symptoms and the disorder's severity, can also affect the possible therapeutic benefits. Despite many unknowns, most care providers do believe that the earlier the child begins intensive intervention, the better the overall result. And the research backs this up. Time and again, researchers point to the benefits of early intervention. But as our discussion moves forward, we will see that there are many obstacles to early intervention. We have already discussed the aspects of diagnosis that can contribute to later intervention, but there are a few other obstacles, including financial, that can also contribute.

Given the diversity of the spectrum and the unique combination of challenges and strengths observed for each child, it is reasonable to believe that no single educational or behavioral approach is going to work for every child. This takes us back to the need to distinguish meaningful subtypes of autism. Essentially, treatments need to be defined based on what symptoms they are affective with based on the specific type of ASD.

Parents of most children are familiar with behavioral methods, using them to modify their child's behavior in some way, such as eliminating tantrums or getting them to stop hitting their siblings. Many child-rearing practices are based on behavioral principles, founded on the belief that you can mold behavior by rewarding desired actions and punishing or ignoring negative ones.

In general, behavioral therapies involve carefully observing current behaviors and then aiming at particular ones for change. Therapists employ a variety of techniques to encourage positive or reduce negative behavior, and continually collecting data on successes and failures. By doing so, they can judge if the child is making significant progress. If not, the therapists can make adjustments to their method. There is a growing body of evidence from these therapists and their hands on trials with their patients. This empirical data is being gathered by the Center for Disease Control (CDC) and being used to create a better overall picture of autism, its symptoms and what appears to be the most affective in providing the children with the skills they need to reach independence in adulthood.

Autistic children often need assistance with verbal skills, social dealings, and challenging activities from head-banging to tantrums to elopement otherwise known as running off. This is probably due to differences in the brain's chemistry, function and structure of individuals with autism. MRIs, which can be used to map the brain, are one tool in the arsenal of researchers who study the brain activity of someone who has autism, versus someone who does not.

Some researchers have suggested a lack of social motivation may be the underlying reason for many of issues these children face. This lack might explain why they do not look into the eyes of others or focus on human faces and voices. It also correlates why those with ASD may fail to develop joint attention, which is looking at or pointing to something, making eye contact with an individual, sharing a mutual enjoyment or interest, and then observing the scene or object together.

Social blindness can lead to a cascade of difficulties because the brain is waiting for important input, including imitation. When the brain doesn't get it, a child may not be able to gain language skills, learn to read emotional cues, pick up social gestures, or have an understanding of the give and take involved in social relationships. Basically, the child is missing critical building blocks for social interaction and educational development because of this missing information.

Fortunately, researchers have begun to understand that an injured or non-developing brain can be put onto the road of repairing itself, through a process of retraining. The reorganization or retraining of brain connections occurs during learning, a key of the repair process. Therefore, behavioral interventions used to treat ASD may not just alter outward behaviors, but may actually support the brain as it rewires itself. Intensive behavioral treatments and interventions can be used to guide the brain in the rewiring process to provide more normal function.

Other traumatic brain injuries have given researchers a chance to study how the brain repairs itself. The information gathered in these studies and observations means that the scientific community is growing in its understanding of how the brain works and how it can be retrained to take over other functions when damage occurs.

Seizures therapy, where a portion of the brain is removed, is one example of the brain taking on the job of repairing and retraining itself. Once the portion is removed, the brain actually functions better. Seizures stop and the sufferer finds that the remaining brain takes over all tasks previously done by both halves. Now let's take that knowledge and awe of the brain back to autism, in the form of a toddler.

For example, if an autistic toddler is uninterested in social interaction, preferring to gaze at inanimate objects rather than at people, a behavioral therapist can aid that toddler acquire pleasure or a sense of reward in gazing at a human face. The more social interaction becomes valuable to the child, the more eye gaze, joint attention, and other fundamental social skills will be able to be nurtured, encouraged, and built upon, assisting developmental progress.

Parents will find themselves being trained by the therapist on how to reinforce the work being done in therapy at home. Following the therapists' instructions is important because this reinforcement can improve a child's overall progress throughout the intervention. Without the family's follow-through, the progress a child makes toward a more normal development can be limited or arrested with no real progress. So what kind of programs are available to those who are looking to behavioral therapy to assist their child in making progress?

There are a number of behavioral approaches, and they can become a confusing alphabet soup to those unfamiliar with them. These are just a few of them: ABA, DTT, PRT, and CBT. Our focus will be ABA and DTT.

Applied Behavior Analysis, or ABA, is the most well-known behavioral intervention. In truth, ABA is an umbrella term, with several specific approaches falling under its general heading. Like everything with autism, there are degrees of effectiveness and variations on different therapies under the ABA umbrella.

One of these is Discrete Trial Training (DTT), which breaks skills or behaviors down into tiny pieces, making a child's accomplishment with each piece more likely. DTT is often used when a therapist is teaching a new skill or behavior, or encourage a behavior that does not happen very often.

So what does this look like in a real life setting? First, the therapist identifies skills or behaviors for intervention. Maybe a child is in their own little world, engaging in repetitive behaviors and not paying attention to people or imitating them. One goal might be to use DTT to inspire imitation.

Usually, the therapist sits across from the child in a quiet space. In a single discrete trial, she encourages imitation by rewarding the child for behaviors such as touching their nose when she touches hers, perhaps by giving praise, a sticker, or a snack. If the child doesn't touch their nose, the therapist may gently prompt them. For example, she might take their hand and help them touch their nose. The therapist carefully chronicles every detail, including what the desired behavior was, if the child did it, whether they needed a prompt, and what reward was received. Then she starts the process over again. This repetition is what helps the child's brain to begin to train itself to be aware of these cues.

Retraining a brain to produce a behavior or to fill in the missing social information is the goal of this therapy. While not every session will meet with a high degree of success, it is the repetition that has proven to be key. Other brain injuries have demonstrated that consistent and repetitive physical therapy can produce consistent and positive results, including the return of function in a damaged limb. It is the documented success of these rewiring efforts that give hope to researchers of autism that the results could be duplicated within this spectrum disorder.

Each time through the process is one discrete trial, and each trial generally takes about 30 seconds. After many discrete trials, the therapist will have a lot of data about whether the child is improving, and which rewards seem to have the best affect. As skills are gained, she can target more complex behaviors for intervention.

ABA is a key feature of most successful intensive early intervention programs. Additional features include a comprehensive curriculum that focuses on imitation, language, toy play, social interaction, motor skills and adaptive behavior. This will also include observing how skills build off of one another and the importance of the behavioral sequence. Parents can really help the therapy sessions by being consistent with the behaviors and rewards at home, while at the same time, following the instructions for reducing interfering behaviors. Gradually, the therapist can help the child transition these behaviors to more natural environments. This type of therapy is very intense, requiring an enormous time commitment, often 25 hours or more per week for at least two years. This therapy can start as early as two years old.

As many families know, getting an ABA program in place for a child can be a challenge. Intensive programs can be time-consuming and pricy. In the U.S., even if a family has medical insurance, that insurance may not cover treatment for autism. In addition, there is a lack of trained ABA therapists available for all the families that need services, depending upon the area. Studies have shown that a family can expect to travel over 40 miles to meet with a behavioral specialist who works with children with autism.

Many early intervention programs, whether home or school based, include elements of ABA or DTT. They also often draw on other key approaches, some of which may be child-led and less structured and restrictive than DTT. With this wide variety of treatment options, the importance of parental involvement can't be underestimated. But with this intensive therapy and parental involvement, the stress on parents can only escalate.

How can extended family and friends help these parents with a diagnosis that alters their lives in many ways? In the next few chapters, we will discuss how that support can be offered in practical ways, while examining what parents can do to help themselves. At the same time, there will be an interjection of the exciting research on the horizon for family dealing with this challenging disorder.

Chapter 5:
What Parents Can Do?

The involvement of parents in their autistic child's life cannot be underestimated. They are the first observers of their child's behavior, noting autistic behaviors long before a doctor might. Then as a treatment plan is developed, the parents commit their time, finances and energy to the treatment plan, as well as reinforcement at home.

Depending on where their child falls on the autistic spectrum, the behavior might require significant changes to the family lifestyle. These parents may feel that it is too difficult to leave their child with other caregivers. Additionally, they deal with their own feelings of sadness when their child will not speak with them or initial loving hugs and affection. As a result, finding out your child has autism can be life-changing. But new findings show parents can still do well emotionally and have a strong bond with their child.

Studies of the coping skills of mothers of autistic children confirm that they are more likely to report poor or fair emotional and mental wellbeing than other moms, but they can also show remarkable strengths. These findings, published in the journal *Pediatrics,* came from a nationally representative survey of almost 62,000 mothers of school-aged children. This study included 364 mothers of autistic children. Researchers concluded that moms of autistic children were just as likely as other moms to report a close relationship with their child and five times as likely report that close relationship than mothers of children with other development disorders not including autism.

Autism and other pervasive developmental disorders (PDD) typically become apparent before age of three. This complex group of developmental disorders can disrupt every part of life, from relationships, physical and emotional health, even an individual's career choices. Here are a few strategies for coping with autism, but also thriving as a family and reaping the joys of parenting your unique child.

First, learn all you can about autism, especially where your child falls on the spectrum. Autism has many variations. As a result, education can help you to understand the potential therapies and how you can be a positive reinforcement for your child. Not every day will be a good day, but knowledge can help you to better understand your child on those bad days.

Secondly, build and keep a social network. This network is a crucial support for parents emotionally and mentally, especially during the stressful periods of time. We will discuss how members of your social network can provide some much needed stress relief later on.

Third, once you have educated yourself, share this knowledge with your family and friends. Help them to better understand some of the behaviors that your child demonstrates and how they can reinforce positive behaviors, while not contributing to negative ones.

Fourth, keep yourself informed about autistic treatments and review them thoroughly before committing your family and child. You are your child's advocate and it's important to be able to make informed decisions.

Fifth, learn about behavioral therapies, specifically the ones involved in your child's treatment plan. Understand that these are not an instant cure, but will assist your child to better manage their autism in the years to come.

Sixth, take the time to learn about the medicinal options, including pharmaceutical ones. It may not be the choice for your family, but be sure to give yourself the knowledge to make an informed decision. This includes looking for credible resources. The internet is full of false information and treatment plans that are designed to part you from your money with no real benefit for your child. Again, your role as the advocate for an autistic child means taking in new treatments being toted on the internet with a grain of salt.

Seventh, be willing to explore diet changes. While not all autistic children have diet issues, changes in the diet that limit certain foods and encourage others may be a good compliment to your child's treatment plan. Even if your child does not suffer from the intestinal issues that can be associated with autism, moving to a healthier diet overall can be beneficial in keeping your child healthy and moving forward. Conversely, large doses of junk food may have an adverse effect on your child's behavior, making them more likely to struggle or easier to trigger their challenging behaviors.

The eighth point is probably one of the most important. Do not be quick to jump into a therapy without doing your research. There are many therapies out there, but many of them are unproven and could present a risk to your child and their progress. At this time, there is no cure for autism, so any therapy promising that should be viewed with suspicion.

Finally, make time for yourself. It's important that parents schedule meaningful breaks for themselves to allow for a recharge. Parents are an important element in a child's life, particularly an autistic child, so it's critical that parents do what they can to reduce their stress through these breaks.

With all those tips, you still have to remember that you must deal with your own feelings. Any parent faced with a diagnosis of autism will wonder what they may have done to cause it. Why my child, they ask themselves in the dark at night. For many, there is not a simple answer. As we have seen, genetics may play a part, but it might not be all there is to it.

Therefore, it's important for parents not to allow themselves to focus so much on finding the place to put blame or fault, but focus on how important your child is to your life and how much they need you to help them to have a great one.

For a moment, stop and look at your child. Study their facial features, their hair, how they cock their head when asking a question. Then list everything about them that just warms your heart. Memorize that list. When the going gets tough (and it will!), recall that list. Sometimes as parents, we can get so caught up in the fight for our child, we don't stop to enjoy their unique contributions to our world and the blessings that they truly are. So make sure that you take a moment each day to count the blessings your child brings to your life. It will be amazing how dwelling on these positive aspects can not only help you to relax and feel better, but that positivity will rub off on your child in a good way.

Learn to look for what autism brings to your child in terms of positives. While we know that autism can results in challenges and struggles, for each individual child, it can also bring increased intelligence or a completely unique perspective of the world. Celebrate what makes your child unique and it will help build their confidence as they face a world that doesn't always understand what autism really means.

The spectrum of autism continues to bring up many questions, both about the causes and effective treatments. So what is on the horizon?

Chapter 6:
The Future of Autism Research

Autism research continues to focus on both causes and treatments, but as we have seen, autism does not receive the research backing that other disorders and diseases do. Various groups, including Autism Speaks, are attempting to change that by funding research grants for doctors and scientists.

Like any disorder or disease, new treatments (both behavioral and pharmaceutical) require years of vigorous testing. Throughout the process, researchers make breakthroughs, but there are also plenty of setbacks. When money isn't available to pay for supplies and research space (including labs and equipment).

When a disorder lacks support from a large share of the population, it can struggle to come up with the necessary dollars to fund research that will make those critical breakthroughs. So how can you support the research for autism, a disorder spectrum which lacks financial backing despite the increasing number of individuals being diagnosed?

If you don't personally have a family member who deals with the challenges of autism, then perhaps you can support a family by using your charitable dollars to support this type of research. Most families with an autistic child find extra money for research support hard to come by. Thus, when you don't have those additional medical costs, it gives you the opportunity to support research. While a few dollars here and there might not seem like much, it can grow into a mighty wave.

Another way to support and encourage research is by your votes. Governmental spending on research is influenced by those voices who speak the loudest. As we have seen with other diseases and disorders, the squeaky wheel gets the grease, or in this case, the research dollars.

But what types of research is being funded? While some looks at causes, others look for treatments. These two have a symbiotic relationship, because when researchers find causes, that research spawns new avenues of investigation for potential treatments. Other types of study include detection tools that can help with diagnosis of autism, thus giving doctors a definitive way to determine where a child lies on the autism spectrum.

Still it is hard to combine the work of these researchers without forums to allow for collaboration. In 2006, all that changed. The Combating Autism Act was passed in the United States Congress. The mission of the act was to provide funding, to the tune of 950 million dollars over five years. Another important part of this act, was the coordination effort. According to the act, the National Institutes of Health (NIH) director was authorized to consolidate and coordinate autism programs to create efficiency, while providing researchers a way to increase their collaboration.

A strategic plan and budget were put into place and as a result, coordination of ASD research began. The Center for Disease Control (CDC) became more active in its monitoring of autism, as well as using grants and collection tools to gather the current information available. The data collected was not just research based, but also information about those who were diagnosed, creating a database where similar symptoms could be discovered. Other areas of the budget were allotted for additional training and better screening tools. Another important was getting information out to the public, allowing for them to be better educated about this disorder.

Overtime, this coordinated effort helped to define areas of critical research and others that would be potential dead ends. Additionally, those who were deemed higher risk, were targeted for early screening and intervention. When disorders and diseases receive this kind of coordination at the federal level, research begins to catch up and offer promising treatments and lines of study. Diagnostic tests and a better understanding of the causes of autism are also being targeted. It's critical to continue the search for the cause, because with that information, early treatment and intervention could arrest this disorder long before a child shows dramatic developmental delays or other struggles and challenges.

In 2011, this act was renewed and received additional funding of over $600 million. During the legislative session of 2014, data was presented in support of renewing the act for another five years with over $1.3 billion in funding. This renewal of the act included key areas previously left out, including money for adult support services, including transition services.

The visit to Congress brought a number of facts to life. One was that there is an extreme shortage of developmental behavioral pediatricians. A child may have to travel over 40 miles or more to see one. Additionally, fewer medical students are choosing to specialize in these pediatric specialty areas, meaning that there are greater geographical disparities as you travel through the nation.

This lack of doctors means that wait times for appointments can be over three months. With a disorder where early intervention is key to a successful outcome, this lack of doctors is disturbing. The CDC and NIH want to change this, by providing incentives for these same medical students to move into these subspecialties.

Some of the research out there includes developing a sensitive tool for measuring behavior change in autistic children. Another course of research is studying cell-type and circuit-specific functional deficits in cortex from gene disruptions linked to autism. All of these directions in research and study are aimed at discovering the cause and the best treatments for autism. Additionally, a better understanding of the cause can lead to clinical tools that provide the illusive early diagnosis.

Another course of scientific study is a recent two-hit model of autism that suggests that as children mature into teenagers, they experience a new wave of social impairments, which is amplified by rapid neural development and socio-affective changes related to puberty. For parents with children aging into adolescence, these areas of research are equally important to how we understand autism throughout the life stages.

While extensive research exists on the foundational social emotional processes during infancy and childhood in ASD, complex social cognition in adolescence has received little attention in the research. Further, the role of hormones in social cognition and ASD is a new area of study. As a result, researchers are looking at how these hormonal and physical changes affect children with autism and if they may regress back from progress they made in their intensive behavioral therapy.

Other studies are being funded in both Europe and the United States dealing with therapies, including looking for the optimal therapy window to have the best success for the children. Interventions are always be studied, tweaked and researched some more as additional information comes to light.

In 2009, scientists discovered that abnormalities in a gene important for learning and memory are a potential cause of autism. The University of Aberdeen finding could hold a key for the future development of autism treatments. In a study published in the *Journal of Medical Genetics*, the researchers explained how their investigations into the gene EIF4E began with the study of one severely autism child. This child was found to have rare re-arrangement of chromosomes and it had disrupted the EIF4E gene. Later, they found additional autistic children who also had these same abnormalities.

In all these cases, an abnormal extra building block in the control region of the gene was found to be disrupting the normal balance of its protein production within the brain cells. The imbalance makes the brain more prone to repetitive thought processes often seen in autism. This opens up a potential target for treatment in the future. EIF4E has an impact on other genes, acting as a gateway for other genetic signals already identified as contributing to autism.

These findings raise the possibility that a correction to the EIF4E abnormalities could improve symptoms of autism, for those whose abnormalities caused autism, but also in those individuals whose autism is caused by the genetic signals that pass through EIF4E.

Once an abnormality is discovered, then scientists can use that information to start creating a test to diagnosis that abnormality consistently. Once such a tool exists, autistic children can be located much earlier, before the development of the typical social delays and other challenges associated with the autism spectrum.

With this exciting research being done, families who live with autism have continued hope for better and more precise treatments and screening tools in the future. Resources are available to families locally and there are chapters of Autism Speaks throughout the country. Families are working to advocate, not only for more research, but also for support for themselves and their children in their communities.

One exciting area of research involves something that parents notice about their children from the day they are born, the eyes. So what do the eyes tell researchers about autism? Let's find out!

Chapter 7:
It's in the Eyes

One unique area of research within the autism community has to do with the eyes, namely the ability of young babies to focus on objects and faces. Researchers have noticed that in 2 to 6 month old babies, where there is a noticeable decline in eye fixation, those children are later diagnosed with autism. This is one of the earliest indicators of delay in social development.

The eyes themselves are a great tool for diagnosing autism, because they are the first sign that a child is not connecting with those around them. Yet, it's interesting that they start out with normal eye fixation, but overtime it declines and this decline may not be easy to discover at first. Combined with other developmental delays over the first two years of life, a doctor can make a diagnosis of autism.

What gives researchers a feeling of progress is that by focusing on the eye fixation, it may be possible to provide even earlier detection of autism. Still that detection can be counterproductive if the treatment options are limited due to lack of resources and personnel.

Currently, almost 80% of children who could benefit by early diagnosis are missed and that window of opportunity creeps shut. So the idea of being able to watch a child's eyes for these early signs could mean an increased chance of diagnosis before that narrow window closes completely. Thus, it is important for doctors, in particular pediatricians, to share this information with the mothers who are pregnant and have newborns. If they are able to alert their doctors early, other development delays can be watched for.

Others argue that children at that age might not be suffering with autism and that may be too early to make such a critical diagnosis. Yet research continually points to the importance of early intervention. If the best time frame for intervention is under 2 years of age, then a diagnosis at the average age of 5 has already missed the critical early intervention window. Thus the outcomes for those children have already been reduced and some therapies may be completely ineffective.

Therefore, any test that gives children a chance at an earlier intervention, the better. However, as we have discussed, there are challenges in reaching professional assistance, even with an early diagnosis. Parents often struggle to get one of those precious appointments with a behavioral therapist or a doctor who works with autism on a regular basis. So even a parent who notices this lack of eye fixation early, they may still have a hard time getting the intervention that they are seeking for their child. This begs the question, do we as a society need to require our pediatricians to be able to perform more of the diagnostic testing, thereby freeing up specialists for treatment? As autism research and testing of treatments continues, this and other ideas will be floated to address this shortage within the medical communities.

So how do parents who have watched their children and received a diagnosis of autism find support? And for extended family members and friends, how can they be a source of encouragement throughout the haul of this lifetime challenge?

Chapter 8:
Support for Families

When it comes to dealing with autism, families need the support of a network, both within the medical community and socially. Family members, in particular the stay at home parent, become the primary caregiver for the autistic child. As a result, while these caregivers understand in theory that they need to take a break, it can be hard to do.

Many worry that they are abandoning their post with their child. Others worry about the reactions of others when their child demonstrates one of their autistic behaviors. Another fear might revolve around their child creating a bond with another adult. This can be particularly acute for the primary caregiver, who may have waited for months or years to hear and feel signs of affection and acknowledgement from their child. If this is denied or gifted to another adult, the parent may feel cheated.

Like the first steps or first word, a parent doesn't want to miss these tentative signs of progress. But if those signs of progress occur with another adult, it can be very difficult for a parent to not take it personally. Their hurt feelings can be a source of depression, especially if they are dwelling on it daily. Getting a caregiver to focus on the positive may be as simple as helping them to find a source of progress from that day, however small it may be. Reframing the day can help them adjust their viewpoint as well, which is a gift every parent can appreciate.

With all that a primary caregiver must do throughout the day, including administering medication, following the therapist's instruction for reinforcement of the child's therapies and caring for other children, it can be even harder for them to see how they can find the time to take a break.

Hence, a social network is critical. If you are a friend or extended family member of someone whose family includes a member with autism, how can you contribute to that social network?

One of the most important ways is by being a good listener. A parent can feel isolated from the rest of the world, because it can be hard to keep up with what's going on in the rest of world while care-giving. They can also feel isolated, because as caregivers, they aren't sure that others understand the challenges their family faces. A family that has a member with autism doesn't just deal with the treatments and endless rounds of doctors' visits, it's also the financial and emotional stress, which can only build over time.

By being a good listener, a friend or extended family member can give that caregiver a chance to unburden their heart. Sometimes just talking through their feelings can help the caregiver of an autistic child feel better about their situation. While listening, keep an ear open for signs of depression or anxiety. Since these individuals are part of their network, they might be able to suggest taking the time for the caregiver to discuss their feelings or thoughts with a mental health professional. It's important to give them support to seek help, before depression or anxiety can drag a caregiver down.

In addition to being a good listener, be one of the individuals to invite their family over for dinner and some fun. Just being out with their autistic child can bring some anxiety, so getting together with friends in a relaxing environment can be helpful to the whole family. Additionally, your acceptance of their child, with all the various and unique aspects they bring, can warm a caregiver's heart.

Whenever possible, provide assistance to the caregiver. Some of the important but simple ways to provide assistance can be providing dinner, thereby taking one chore off the caregiver's list. Other ways to provide assistance could be by volunteering to watch the kids and give the parents a night out. Even giving a parent two hours to do errands without the whole compliment of children can feel like a vacation. As it's often been said, the little things mean a lot. For families with autistic children, it is these small gestures that can relieve stress and give them a much needed boost.

Little things, from grabbing a few groceries while you are already at the store to helping mow the lawn, can be great ways to take one thing off the caregiver's packed list. While it won't take all the stress away, these tips can help a friend or extended family member keep the caregiver from feeling isolated and overwhelmed.

In addition to providing this type of assistance as part of the social network, show support through your backing of research. Walks and other events to raise money for therapies and research can be a great source of encouragement to families with an autistic child. Here they see that their family isn't alone in dealing with the blessings and challenges of this disorder spectrum.

Now let's look at the medical network. In a world where the research shows that the number of doctors available is limited, it can be hard to build a quality medical network where your child receives all the necessary care. So how can you do so?

Take the time to speak with your doctors. Learn the terminology, so that you can better understand what your doctor is telling you. Doing your own homework can help you to refine your question prior to meeting with the doctor. Also, don't be afraid to take notes throughout your appointments, so you can refer back to them at a later time. There will be days when you are tired and can't remember what was discussed, so those notes will come in handy.

Points about your child's treatment can be confusing, so don't hesitate to ask questions or even sit in on your child's sessions. It gives you a resource for encouraging the same positive behaviors at home. The medical staff want to help you, but remember, they have multiple families to work with. So you have to remain your child's greatest advocate. Be prepared to be your own secretary. Consider building a binder with your notes and a compiled medical record for your child. This will be a great resource for when or if you are transferred to a different doctor or other medical professional.

Autism Speaks is a national organization geared toward financing research through grants, as well as advocating for those with autism and their families. This organization provides support groups, where parents can go to talk with others who are dealing with the same issues and concerns. They have groups all over the country.

Parents are encouraged to add a support group with an autism focus to their medical war chest. These organizations can help parents to stay up to date with the latest research, diagnosis methods and how various legislation is progressing, particularly in the areas of insurance coverage consistent across the states. This advocacy is important, because for many, autism therapy can be the straw that breaks a family's financial back.

Chapter 9:
The Financials of Autism

When a family receives a diagnosis of autism, the first thought is to find the best therapy available and begin treatment to give their child the best outcome. Then the first of the bills begins to arrive. These medical bills can get extensive rather quickly, as the specialists are rare and therefore, costly. In addition, these specialists and therapists are typically not close by, so travel costs are incurred as well. Bills can quickly pile up. Unfortunately, this spectrum disorder is not uniformly covered under health insurance plans, greatly increasing the financial burden for families. Additionally, most families can't afford for the autistic child to go to a daycare program in addition to the therapy and other activities, so one parent may be forced to stay home, further reducing the family's income at a time when they need it the most.

From state to state, what therapies and diagnosis screenings are covered and available can vary dramatically. ABA treatment, for example, is a behavioral treatment that involves positive reinforcement for various behaviors, while discouraging negative behaviors. It has been proven that this is an effective treatment, but the coverage varies dramatically from Medicaid to private health insurance. Currently, only 37 states require private insurance to cover autism and under federal health plans only 20 states provide this coverage. Even with coverage, the co-pays and deductibles can still be a substantial burden to the family as they make other changes in their lifestyle to accommodate the needs of their autistic child.

As you can see, it is this lack of coverage that can inhibit the forward progress of a child with autism. Their parents shoulder a great financial responsibility without any definitive cure or treatment. While much progress has been made and more treatments are being identified, the ability to pay for them is not available.

Advocacy groups continue to work from state to state, trying to change the laws to make sure that the insurance coverage is available for families with autistic children. Another area of concern is for the children who have become adults. Treatments may be ongoing into adulthood, yet the insurance coverage may not be available to them that covers these treatments. If the insurance is available, the out of pockets costs in the form of deductibles and co-pays can burden this adult child in much the same way it did their parents, but they lack any financial resources, unlike their parents.

As a result, parents may continue to help their adult children shoulder this financial responsibility. Thus autism can persistently cripple families economically across the generations.

Currently, roughly 3% of autistic children are uninsured. However, one in three children diagnosed with autism receive exclusive coverage through a Medicaid or CHIP program. Over 50% of children with autism use Medicaid or CHIP to provide partial insurance coverage for their medical expenses. Without this social safety net, many of these children would be left with no ability to pay for necessary treatment and parents would be left to make hard choices between other expenses and treatment.

So what does Medicaid cover for these autistic children? For most, Medicaid covers the initial screenings and treatments under its mandatory services. Other facets provide waivers to allow for optional services. Those optional services and their availability vary from state to state.

But autism has a greater financial impact than just on the individual families of those with an autistic child. Society pays for autism to the tune of $137 billion a year just in the United States alone. An individual family can expect roughly $3.5 million in costs over the lifetime of their autistic child. Now imagine that number being doubled or even tripled. For families with one autistic child, they have a greater than 20% chance of having another one. So the financial burden for a family can only increase when multiple children are diagnosed. Yet with early intervention, that lifetime cost can be reduced by two-thirds, making it worthwhile for governments to invest in early intervention for those diagnosed.

Here's another important factor to consider. While autism strikes across all ethnic, racial and socioeconomic backgrounds, those who live in underprivileged areas are more likely to be diagnosed later and struggle to find the proper treatment services. Additionally, due to the lack of personnel, their families will often have to travel further to receive treatment, which increases their overall financial burden and of course this is a source of considerable stress for the family as a whole.

Currently the average diagnosis age is 5 years old, but again, those whose parents are aware of warning signs and are able to provide the wellness visits that give the best opportunity for early diagnosis. This is been considered a missed opportunity to provide early diagnosis and treatment.

The window of opportunity to provide change for autism is within the first two years of a child's life. The best outcome occurs when intervention takes place in that window of opportunity. One of the ways that intervention can take place is through community involvement. Using such programs as

Headstart to screen children as well as being a point of contact for parents to learn more and for treatment services to be provided is just one way for early intervention and the benefits to occur.

In the future, researchers hope that the autism outcome is early intervention allowing adults to live independent lives as working adults with families of their own. So how does autism look as a child ages? And are their pitfalls for an autistic child when it comes to dealing with their peers as teenagers? Let's look at how autism and drug use can combine to the detriment of an autistic teenager.

Chapter 10:
Drug Use and Autism

In dealing with autism, children who have been diagnosed struggle with understanding the social cues of their peers. Being a teenager is hard enough, but it can be extremely difficult without an ability to understand social cues. As a result, some kids with higher functioning autism will struggle with fitting in and may not make wise choices as a result.

Understand, as teenagers, all of us struggled with making choices, especially since our ability to predict the long term consequences had not caught up with us yet. Autistic kids stand out beyond the normal differences of teenagers, almost like having a target on their back for teasing and bullying. All of us remember times where we felt like we didn't fit in with group. Now imagine that big target on your back. It would just make the situation worse. Since autistic children are prone to depression, this teasing can contribute to a bout with depression and feelings of being socially incapable.

Since these kids aren't necessarily able to judge the consequences, they may feel that using drugs and alcohol will help them to fit in with their peers. AT the same time, they might feel more in control after a beer, creating a false self-confidence. The result can be a self-medication, as many others do when dealing with health issues or mental distress. As society has seen time and again, this way of dealing with health and mental trauma can be extremely harmful in the long run.

So what are the dangers of substance abuse for those with autism? For one thing, the ability to make sound choices in this regard are affected by the autism, this making it hard for them to use alcohol and other drugs in a safe and sensible way. The pitfall is their lack of social skills and insight, so they cannot make good decisions about what is appropriate behavior, depending on the context of the situation.

The effects on their brains might be different as well. The result is that these same drugs may be more dangerous for the autistic brain than others. Overdosing or other reactions may be more pronounced in an autistic individuals. So what can parents do if they suspect their child of using or abusing alcohol and drugs?

The first thing is to consult a professional with an autism background to provide assistance. They can aid a family to the help that makes the most sense for their child, while acknowledging how their autism can play a part in their struggle, providing another layer of challenges.

An interesting study was conducted in London, looking specifically at the hereditary factors involved in alcohol abuse. A specific gene associated with autism, known as the AUTS2, was studied to see if it had any ties to alcoholism. The researchers found that this gene was part of a significant association between this gene and alcohol over ingestion. By studying this gene, researchers are one step closer to understanding alcoholism and its hereditary possibilities, but also begin to build a greater knowledge of how autism can be passed down within families.

The association between this gene and alcohol could also be a basis for a potential therapy for alcohol abuse. In addition, a greater awareness of this gene can help researchers to begin to unravel how it affects autism. The connection may mean that those with autism need to avoid alcohol because they might be more likely to suffer the effects of alcohol abuse.

These studies recognize that those young children grow up and they have all the challenges of becoming teenagers and adults, along with the challenges inherit in autism. So what does life for an autistic individual look like throughout the years? And how do they achieve their own support system to help them with the challenges that will come as they age with this unique spectrum disorder? The following chapter will look at autism throughout an individual's life.

Chapter 11:
Autism throughout Life

Autism is often associated with children. The focus for many is on early detection and intervention with therapies, geared at assisting these children to lead productive lives as adults.

Yet, these children do grow up and become adults with autism. Their ability to function in society can be enhanced due to early intervention, but they may continue to face challenges, especially as they age and their hormones and other body chemicals fluctuate.

In addition, the support systems that are available to families with an autistic child are not necessarily available to the adult autistic individual. With an increase in our understanding of autism and this disorder spectrum, diagnosis has risen for children. But again, these children will grow up and require systems that encourage them to continue to progress, while dealing with challenges both from their disorder and those naturally occurring due to aging.

As anyone with a long term disorder or physical challenge will tell you, life changes affect them too. Aging effects not only their bodies, but can have an effect on their disorder, not necessarily in a positive way. As a result, their quality of life relies not just on the foundation provided in childhood, but also on the support received throughout their adult years. Specific areas of support can include educational, medical, social, family and employment needs.

Various autism societies and organizations provide this type of support throughout an autistic individual's lifetime, which can be divided into three critical life stages. These include childhood and early development, adolescence and finally adulthood.

Starting in Childhood: Creating a Foundation

When it comes to childhood autism, the key is early intervention. As we have explored in our discussion of autism, this early intervention has been found to be helpful in providing the brain new patterns to follow and allowing these children to learn how to overcome or use specific behaviors to cope with their disorder.

Autistic behaviors, including delayed development and a lack of social interaction, can appear as early as 18 months, so parents are encouraged to tell their pediatrician as soon as they detect any delays. Thankfully, pediatricians are being trained to look for these developmental delays, so it's important to be honest with your pediatrician throughout the early wellness visits, which are spaced relatively close together for the first two years of life.

By beginning treatments early in your child's life, the costs of autism can reduced by as much as two-thirds. Why is early treatment so effective in reducing lifetime costs? Simply put, the early intervention allows for behavioral therapy to have the greatest impact, while teaching an autistic child how to manage their disorder effectively throughout their lifetime.

Additionally, with a childhood diagnosis, parents have the greatest chance of accessing the necessary support for their family, while learning everything they can about their family member's place on the autism spectrum. This support system will continue to be affective as they move into the next stage.

Adolescence: Building on the Foundation

When diagnosis doesn't occur until later in life, that foundation of knowledge, therapy and coping skills are not put in place, making it harder for an older child or adult to have the same positive outcomes from therapy or other interventions.

For adolescence, it's important to keep building on the foundation achieved throughout childhood. This means continuing affective treatments or building to new, more comprehensive ones. In addition, educational programs can help the adolescent reach their potential through creativity when dealing with the challenges of the disorder.

At the same time, it's important to remember that hormones are changing for teenagers. What therapies and medicines were affective in the past, might not be as affective with a teenager. Therefore, it is important to talk with your doctor about any changes you see occurring with your child. There may need to be adjustments to their therapies or medications.

While dietary changes may not be affective for everyone, as a child moves into their teenage years, maintaining healthy eating habits and minimizing the not-so healthy options can only help their bodies maintain balance of growth and hormones.

As they move through school levels, adolescents can be helped to prepare for a transition to independent adult living, imparting skill sets these kids will need. Here is an area where you can be your child's cheerleader. As they try new things for the first time, your child won't always be successful. Help them to appreciate that the failures are just as important as the successes. Use those failures to help them tweak their coping mechanisms or make adjustments to their therapies to assist them in better handling of those situations in the future.

Remember, your adolescent is going through a variety of changes, both in terms of their bodies, their brain development and new social demands that didn't exist in the past (dating for example). On top of this, at a time when the acceptance of their peers is paramount, they have a disorder that makes them stand out and not always in a positive way.

So your support and encouragement will definitely be needed. Make sure you are a listening ear and working with your child to manage their disorder. They will appreciate you treating them as an individual with a disorder, versus just their autism.

Adulthood: The Final Frontier

Adulthood means moving into a different stage of life. For many teenagers, this will be their first time living away from home and being totally responsible for themselves. If your child is autistic, this is a dream that you continually hope they can achieve. Yet, some children may never be able to be completely independent. When that is the case, the caregiver's support system will continue to be vitally important, as the responsibilities of caring for an adult will differ from a child or even an adolescent.

Independent living is the ultimate goal, but for those who might not achieve it, providing independence in a variety of areas can contribute to the quality of life for adults with autism. However, if your child is able to live independently, your role may be reduced but you are still a vital part of their network. Your support and encouragement will need to continue, even as they move out on their own.

Studies have found that landing within the autism spectrum disorder range can lead to a diagnosis of other mental illnesses. Doctors and researchers are not sure if this is due to the alterations in the brain, which have already occurred in the case of autistic children, or if it is due to the stress and struggles resulting from dealing with the challenges of autism. Still, the research has proven that there is some connection between autism and an increased likelihood of a mental illness.

The numbers can be frightening, with roughly 40% of those diagnosed with autism suffering from depression. Another 9% will suffer from either schizophrenia or bi-polar disorder. For parents, this can be a scary prospect. Not only do they have to battle with all the challenges of autism, but then they have to worry about these other potential illnesses and the setbacks they can present to their child.

For adults with autism, it's important to stay close to those who know you best and can help you seek assistance, particularly at the first signs of depression. This is the mental illness most likely to show its face and with the stress and anxiety that autism can produce, it is easy to see why depression is so prevalent.

Parents need to encourage their adult autistic children to practice self-advocacy. After all, they are in the best position to understand what they have experienced, their needs and how this affects their identities. This can help them to find services to assist them. Additionally, teach them how to confer with their doctors and be their own medical advocate. As they age, their autism will be part of their medical history and it's important that they understand their meds, therapies and any dietary restrictions they have decided to follow, as this will contribute to how doctors chose treatments them in the future.

The Autism Society works for autistic adults by helping them to access services and support systems that will help them to maximize their own independence in whatever settings they might find themselves. They also focus on helping these adults to achieve the highest quality life available to them. By encouraging your child to maintain their intellectual activities, they can maintain their progress in dealing with the challenges of autism. At the same time, those adults will blaze a trail for those coming after them, showing that there can be a successful adult life with autism.

Conclusion

The work in the field of autism continues to grow, but as with so many disorders and diseases, progress has been slow. While therapies have been developed, the actual cause of autism still alludes researchers.

We have covered a broad range of information on autism. This spectrum of disorders is very focused on the social, emotional and developmental aspects of behavior in children. Yet, within this spectrum there is a broad range of severity, and it can be paired with other unrelated disorders.

The spectrum is wide and has a lot of variables. What is interesting is that these disorders don't come with a simple blood test, but must be diagnosed through observation and a set of defined behavioral perimeters. Parents are critical to this process, because they have the most interaction with their children. If they notice developmental delays, it's important to let your doctor know during your typical wellness visits. The younger a child is diagnosis the better chance that therapeutic intervention will have a positive effect.

While each child is different, the same is also true about therapies. Not all of them are affective with each child. Within the therapeutic community, it can be difficult to demonstrate a therapy working consistently again and again, making it hard to establish a proven therapy. At the same time, researchers have found that certain behavioral therapies may not always transfer skills to the autistic individual for use outside of the therapy setting. Tailoring a plan with your child's therapist is important for any successful therapy.

Research has made many promising breakthroughs, including finding genes with abnormalities that contribute to autism.

This research is moving closer to finding not only the causes of autism, but also better treatments and therapies. Additionally, by narrowing down the causes of autism, better diagnostic testing can be developed.

Early intervention continues to be the key to making any progress in reversing the developmental delays associated with autism. While it isn't a cure, therapy can help autistic children to continue to make the kind of progress that will allow them to move toward an independent lifestyle.

But with every move forward, parents have to deal with the potential setbacks. These can be financial in nature, which can create a large amount of stress on the family, particularly if they don't live in a state that mandated insurance companies cover autism treatments.

Other sources of stress and conflict could be the constant travel and strain of doctor's visits falling on the chosen caregiver. Extended family can play a great part in helping to ease the burden by helping with everyday chores, babysitting or providing entertainment in a way that makes the family including their autistic member feel accepted.

As a child with autism ages, new challenges will arise. Parents need to be on the lookout for other symptoms of mental illnesses, such as depression. While all parents have to teach their children about the use of drugs and alcohol, autistic children need even more intervention in this regard. Their ability to make sound choices might be limited, so parents need to be even more vigilant.

Still at the end, an autistic child can achieve a level of independence with their parents' guidance and support. Researchers are studying the causes and treatments for autism, but they are also looking at how successful autism adults are with early intervention. As each generation grows older, they provide data that researchers can study to refine treatments and that can point them to potential lines of study for a cause.

Throughout our tour of autism, we have learned a lot about the spectrum, treatment through therapy and some promising areas of research. But we also discussed some of the myths about autism. The biggest myth is that autistic individuals lack emotions, when in fact they lack a connection with individuals because they do not pick up on social cues and then translate them correctly. While it can be a learned behavior for these children, it may never be truly natural for them the way it is for most of us.

We also discussed one of the biggest debates in the world of autism, that of vaccines and their connection, or lack of one, with autism. While research continues to show no causal relationship between autism and vaccines, the lack of a confirmed cause of autism means that this debate will rage onward. Parents who choose not to vaccinate to avoid the potential tie to autism may be exposing their children to a wide variety of diseases. It's important to discuss the vaccines on your child's schedule with your doctor and educate yourself so you can make an informed choice about vaccines.

As with everything autism, continuing research will answer many questions. However, this disorder spectrum is not heavily studied. Groups of parents, patients and scientists are working to increase the research dollars for autism. Support groups have also grown up to assist parents and families in finding resources to assist them with therapy costs and the stress that can build up in a family dealing with autism.

Wake-Up Call

Finally, it's important to remember that a diagnosis of autism can be a huge financial burden on a family because most insurance companies do not cover autism. There are various groups that are working on changing the laws state by state to have these costs included as part of basic medical coverage. So family members who may have received an autism diagnosis are dealing not only with treatment but also a financial burden as well. Sometimes the best support you can offer a family with an autistic child is to give the parents a much needed break in order to help them recharge from the stress that this diagnosis can put on their family.

In the end, it's important to understand that autism isn't a horrible diagnosis, but it is one that will require a lot from family and caregivers to help these special children achieve their potential.

Click to participate in Autism crowd funding projects:

Kickstarter.com

Indiegogo.com

GoFundMe.com

Emotional Intelligence

Develop and apply improved social skills and take control of relationships in your life

TABLE OF CONTENTS

Chapter 1:
Developing Emotional Intelligence

Do you have emotional intelligence? The truth is that everyone has some level of what is referred to as emotional intelligence – some people just have more of it than others. If you are lacking emotional intelligence, luckily you can learn to develop more of it and use it in your everyday life. But first, how do you know whether you have a lot of emotional intelligence, or only a little? In order to answer this, you will first have to understand what emotional intelligence is.

Emotional intelligence is all about being able to know what people around you are feeling – what their emotions are. People with high emotional intelligence can easily tell what people they are associating with are feeling, and can then use it to benefit both themselves and others. If you understand what others are feeling, you will know how to treat them, talk to them, successfully work with them, and so much more.

You are probably wondering how you can develop your emotional intelligence. Well, you need to try to be more aware of your surroundings. Next time you are around others, try to take in all the little things about them that can signify what they are feeling. Are you someone who is generally caught up in a million things at once? Are you often stressed, worried, and frazzled? If this sounds like you, then you might be having trouble developing emotional intelligence because you don't take the time to focus on what is going on around you - you are always caught up in other things.

To develop your emotional intelligence, try practicing mindfulness. Mindfulness is just focusing on the present – instead of what might happen in the future or what has happened in the past. It sounds so simple, doesn't it? However, the truth is that with all the distractions of life, putting it into practice can be another story entirely.

You will have to work at it – so don't be discouraged if at first you fail. Practice again and again, and you will find yourself getting better at truly living in the present moment. In order to practice mindfulness, it is essential to be calm. So, you may need to do some breathing exercises to get rid of any stress or anxiety. This will hopefully allow you to be calm enough to focus on only what is going on around you, instead of worrying needlessly about other things.

How will this new skill called mindfulness help you develop your emotional intelligence? Well, if you practice mindfulness when you are around others, you will be able to easily pick up on their emotions. You will be focused on the present, which make you a lot less likely to miss a sudden change in, for example, someone's face or voice. It is the little signs like these that can tell you how someone is feeling – and in order to notice them, you need to be completely focused on what is going on around you.

Hopefully these tips will help you develop more emotional intelligence in no time. To quickly summarize the key points of this chapter, be sure to remember how important it is to get rid of stress so you can focus on the present. This will increase your emotional intelligence greatly. But, now that you have greater emotional intelligence, you need to learn how to apply it in everyday life. If correctly applied, emotional intelligence can be extremely helpful. Keep reading to learn how to apply emotional intelligence in your life. Emotional intelligence can help you develop and sustain the relationships you have always wanted. With emotional intelligence, you will have more control over the relationships in your life. If you want to improve a relationship that you feel needs work, you will be able to. If you want to mend a friendship, it won't be as hard. Your family and work life will greatly benefit from your new skill – so don't wait any longer! The next chapter of this book will help you on your journey to improving the relationships in your life.

Chapter 2:
Applying Emotional Intelligence

In the last chapter you learned how to develop more emotional intelligence. Hopefully you are starting to apply these tips and ideas in your own life – but you may be having some trouble with that. Maybe you don't know exactly how to apply emotional intelligence to you everyday life. Well, applying emotional intelligence is just about learning how to use it to help you develop and grow relationships to their full potential.

So, to apply your newly developed emotional intelligence, you will need to first think about the situations that it will be useful in. So, think about this: are there any relationships in your life that you need to improve and work on? Is there any area in your life where you are having trouble with relationships: whether this may be personal or professional? The first step to developing these relationships is recognizing what situations require emotional intelligence, and what situations require you to use more emotional intelligence than others.

So, think about the situations that you encounter in day to day life which could be made easier if you were to simply apply some emotional intelligence. What interactions with others are difficult? What relationships are faltering or even falling apart? Now you know where to apply emotional intelligence. The next step is to know how to apply it to the specific situation.

In order to apply emotional intelligence, you will need to recognize these situations and then remember to take others' emotions into consideration when you are in these specific situations. Some situations will call for more emotional intelligence than others. These are situations where you are really struggling – but with emotional intelligence, you will find a way to work out these problems in no time at all.

For example, if you are always arguing with someone, and can sense your relationship with them is gradually deteriorating, this is a situation where emotional intelligence can be a great help. With emotional intelligence, you can take the steps to gradually mend your relationship and become a happier, healthier person as a result.

First, take a step back from the situation and think about how you can apply emotional intelligence for the benefit of the relationship. Then, try to really focus on understanding what the other person is feeling and going through. Try as hard as you can to read their subtle voice tones, body language, reactions, and anything else, so you can figure out what emotions they are experiencing.

So, what do you do once you have some sort of idea of their emotions? The next step is to use this new knowledge to treat them accordingly, talk to them in a way that is best considering what their emotion is at the moment, and just interact with them in a way that takes their emotions into consideration. So, for example, if they seem to be having a very hard day, you would talk to them in a tone that might make them feel better. Of course, this is only one example – you will have to figure out how to apply your emotional intelligence to the specific situations that have occurred or will occur in your everyday life.

My hope is that now that you know more about how to apply emotional intelligence, you will find ways to strengthen the relationships in your life and build new ones that you never would have been able to build before. Between the information from this chapter and the information included in the last, you already know a lot about emotional intelligence and how you can use it in terms of relationships.

In the next two chapters, we will get more specific and delve into two particular categories of relationships. This will help you to learn about situations on a more specific and case by case level – but of course, in the end you will still have to tailor all of this knowledge to fit your own unique circumstances.

The next chapter will focus on how you can use emotional intelligence in your personal relationships. You will learn how you can start helping these relationships right now by simply applying the emotional intelligence that you have developed. In this chapter, the focus will be specifically on family relationships. This will include relationships with both members of your immediate family and your extended family.

Chapter 3:
Emotional Intelligence and Personal Relationships

In order to have the best kind of relationships in your life, you need emotional intelligence. In the past chapters you learned what emotional intelligence is and in general how it can be applied. In this chapter, you will learn specifically how you can apply it to benefit the relationships that you have in your personal life.

I am going to start broadly and talk about extended family. First, you will learn how to use emotional intelligence to take control of relationships with people you may not see as often. So, have you been having trouble with your relationship with, for example, your grandmother or mother? Or are you having trouble relating to your brother-in-law or brother who lives across the country – or maybe even across the world? How can you start to mend these relationships so that you can finally have the kind of interaction with these people that you have dreamed of for so long?

Well, the answer is quite simple. It is emotional intelligence: with emotional intelligence you can take control of these family relationships, so that everyone will be happier. There is no need to continue living full of stress, worry, and feelings of sadness because these relationships just did not work out. If you want to get closer to these people in your life, now you can!

First, figure out what relationships in your life you would like to work on. Think about which relationships are leaving you feeling unhappy because they have not worked out. Figure out which relationships could help you to be a happier person if they were different. Then, act on your wish to mend these relationships. You can just start with one relationship if you do not want to take on too much at one time.

Next, start reaching out to the person that you want to build your relationship with. If you are already planning to see them, don't stress out or worry – even if this is what you normally do. When you see them, or when you talk to them over the phone, try to gauge their emotions. Try to be aware of what they are feeling, and how they are reacting to what you are saying to them – even to just seeing you in general. Your words, actions, and reactions should all depend on how you see them behaving. The way they behave is a great way to tell what they are feeling inside. If you are experienced at reading people's emotions, you will be able to easily figure out how they are feeling and then use this knowledge to both of your benefits. They will benefit from your emotional intelligence as well. Since you are using emotional intelligence, you will be less likely to have a misunderstanding, or say something to them that they will interpret in the wrong way. And, even better, you will be more likely to meet and talk again soon. With emotional intelligence, you are well on your way to building a stronger, healthier relationship with this family member – even if you feel like you don't know them that well because you don't see them every day (or even every year).

The truth is that extended family relationships can be hard to maintain for these very reasons – you just don't know them as well as your other family members. For this reason, it is especially important that all your attention and focus in on them during those few hours each month, or maybe each year, that you get to spend with them. In our busy lives, it is far too often that our attention is elsewhere – making it possible to use emotional intelligence in these situations.

You need to fully focus on the person you are talking to and spending time with, so that you can make up for lost time. Maybe there is something that has happened in their lives since you have last seen them that you don't even know about. Well, the truth is that maybe you are never going to find out about it. Or, at least you are not going to find about all of the details that the people closer to this person know. However, that doesn't mean that you can't read and figure out generalizations about what has gone on from their face, their voice, and their actions – and sometimes, to be honest, that is all you need to know. With this knowledge, you can better understand their actions. It will help you not to lash out at them if you understand the motives for their behavior or harsh words. And it will help you to treat them the way you yourself would want to be treated if you were in their situation – to say the things that will help them through whatever it is that they are going through.

Next, let's think about the relationships with the people you see every day. These relationships encounter plenty of problems of their own. You can build back up a broken relationship by trying to understand what the other person is feeling, and by using this knowledge to interact with them accordingly. For example, take someone who is always fighting with their spouse. In this case, it may be that the two people are not reading each other's emotions correctly. In order to mend the situation, a good first step would be for them to pay attention to the other person's emotions.

In all family relationships, you may have to assess the situation and see if you are focusing on yourself too much. Perhaps you are just wrapped up in worry about your own problems. Or maybe you are worried about what other people think about you. The truth is that in order to have better relationships with these people, you will have to stop focusing on yourself and start focusing on them. You can focus on yourself and them – the interactions you are having together. This will make it harder to misread their face or voice, which is exactly what you want. You want to be able to read them correctly so you know how to act around them and how to talk with them.

Taking control of the personal relationships in your life is all about helping relationships to work so that you can be happy again. It is all about taking your thoughts about what you want the relationships in your life to be like – and making these hopes and dreams become a reality. With a higher emotional intelligence, you can do this easily. In fact, you probably won't believe how easy it is with emotional intelligence.

Right now, you might be thinking that there are other relationships in your life as well – so what about those? These relationships are very different from the relationships that you have with your family. Probably the other largest category of relationships, the one that most people can relate to, are the relationships you have with the people you work with. These professional relationships can be difficult as well – especially if you are in a tough work situation, or a job that you don't really like. But no matter what, knowing how to take control of these professional relationships is very important. In the next chapter, you will learn how emotional intelligence can help you with this.

Chapter 4:
Emotional Intelligence and Professional Relationships

Now you are going to learn how a higher emotional intelligence can help your relationships with your boss and your coworkers. First, let's talk about your boss or supervisor at work. This relationship is obviously very important – and one that you don't want to mess up. Sometimes, this relationship can be very hard – you are trying to act the right way, but one little mistake can send you worrying that your job might be on the line.

So, to prevent this excess worrying, you will need to acquire some emotional intelligence. If you can tell what your boss is thinking and feeling, then even if they aren't saying it you will have a better idea of what is happening. This will prevent you from thinking you are getting fired when in reality they are just having a bad day. It is important to understand people's emotions because these emotions will show in their faces – and you don't want to jump to the wrong conclusion that these emotions are because of you.

Emotional intelligence is all about focusing on what is going on around you – in specific the other people around you and anything about them that could tell you how they are feeling. This is very important in the work situation – there are a lot of people and your ability to interact with them may mean the difference between keeping the job you love and losing it. So how can having more emotional intelligence help you to successfully interact with your coworkers in a way that is both productive and right for the specific job situation you are in? Well, there are so many ways which emotional intelligence can help you interact with coworkers. If you are working as a group with other employees, it is time to make sure you are using your emotional intelligence to the best of your abilities – because you are definitely going to need it.

Prior to this we have basically been talking about relationships where only two people are involved. Now, in the workplace, we are talking about social situations where you are required to work with multiple people – whether this means several people or a whole group. So, what does this mean in terms of using emotional intelligence? Well, unfortunately this means that it is going to be much harder. The reason you will likely find it more difficult is that you simply have more people around you, which means you have more emotions and feelings to try to gauge to the best of your ability.

This just means that it is even more important than before to practice mindfulness and to learn to come to the workplace completely stress-free. If you are not stressed, it will be so much easier to use your emotional intelligence when you are in a group of people. You also need to completely focus on what is going on around you in order to practice emotional intelligence around more than one person. If you have developed these skills which were outlined earlier in the book, it will make it so much easier to work with others. Working with others requires that you understand their emotions because if you can't you either won't know how to interact with them, or, more likely, you will interact with them in the wrong way.

If someone is having a bad day, or something has just happened in your life, then you will need to adjust the way you talk to them accordingly. The failure to do this can result in difficulty working as a group, arguments, or even a fight. However, if you can do this, then the group will work so much more smoothly. Everything will go smoothly because you all are taking the time to understand each other, and to tailor interactions to each specific person depending on the way that person is interacting with you. It is important to be able to look at a person and decide quickly how you should interact with them to achieve the results you want – which in this case is harmony throughout the group which will allow you all to work together and get the job done.

If you are a supervisor at work, whether you are just supervising a small group for a simple project or a larger number of people for a long time, then emotional intelligence is especially important. Without emotional intelligence, how will you ensure that everything with the group is running smoothly? You will get so much work done if you have higher emotional intelligence. Remember, if you don't feel like you currently have a high emotional intelligence, there is no need to fret. Earlier in this book tips were given for how to successfully develop your emotional intelligence. So no matter how lacking you feel that you are in this area, these tips will be just the help that you need. Follow them to have more emotional intelligence in no time – and all the relationships in your life will benefit from it.

In this chapter you learned some tips for using emotional intelligence to help you navigate the difficulties of the workplace. In the last chapter, you learned about using emotional intelligence when at home for the benefit of the relationships that you have there. Now, in the last chapter of the book, we will be talking about emotional intelligence and social skills in general. You will learn how to use your emotional intelligence to have better social skills. So, do you feel that your social skills could use improvement? Well, if you do, then this will be an important section for you. Emotional intelligence will help you to interact with all types of people better.

Chapter 5:
Emotional Intelligence and Social Skills

In the last chapters you have been learning about how to interact with people you know – whether that means close family members or at least people you know of and have seen before. However, that seems to give the impression that emotional intelligence can only be beneficial to relationships you have with people that you already know – however well you may know them. The truth is that emotional intelligence can actually help with any social interaction – even if you don't have an actual relationship with the person and never will. What do I mean by this? Well, let's give some quick examples from everyday life that most people can probably relate to.

If you are, for example, at the store and interacting with a stranger, then emotional intelligence can help. If you are going to see a doctor, emotional intelligence can help. Emotional intelligence can help with all social interactions that you have with anyone, anywhere. If you have emotional intelligence, you can use it to develop your social skills.

So, in what way are you looking to develop your social skills? Are you hoping to have an easier time deciding how to interact with a specific person or type of person? Do you want new social situations to be smoother for you – you want to minimize worrying about them even though they are something you have never experienced before? Or do you want to know what to say in difficult social situations when it seems there are just no words? Well, emotional intelligence can help you in all of these situations.

With emotional intelligence, you will know what to say and how to behave – no matter how foreign the situation is. You will know how to interact with different types of people – and how to decide to interact with someone that you are about to meet. You will also know how to stop worrying about new situations and experiences. How can emotional intelligence help with all of this? Well, it really is simple. As you have already learned, emotional intelligence helps you to tell what other people's emotions are. And in all of these situations, what you really need is to be able to know what the other person is feeling. If you know this, then the interaction will come so much more naturally. Emotional intelligence truly is a wonderful skill to have in these situations!

So, let's start with the first situation and elaborate just a little so that you can get a better idea of this. Is there a specific person that you are having trouble knowing how to interact with? If this is the case, then you can stop worrying about it. Simply use your emotional intelligence when you are in a situation with this person. Try to read their emotions, and interact accordingly. With emotional intelligence, even if you have never met this person before the interaction will still be smooth. Even if you don't get along with this specific type of person, with emotional intelligence, you will be able to make things go better than they normally would. Try to understand them, and think about where they are coming from. Forget everything else you are thinking about, and focus your attention on them, and how you think it would be best to interact with them. This will be sure to help turn an uncomfortable situation into a much more comfortable one.

Next, are you worrying about a social situation because it is new and different? Emotional intelligence will help you to get through even the newest of situations. It is all about being able to learn about the people you are with, even if you have never met them. How do you use emotional intelligence to learn about them? Well, you need to try to read their emotions.

Emotions can be deducted based on how they are speaking, how they look (happy, sad, uncomfortable, nervous) and so much more. If you look closely enough, you can learn about someone you have never met. It is definitely possible – you just have to be focused and you have to be living in the present moment.

Now, let's talk a little about the last scenario that was posed as a question above. This scenario involves difficult social situations when it seems there are no words to say. In a situation like this, it will be extremely important to try to figure out the other person's emotions. Then, you will know what to say based on how they seem to be feeling. All in all, emotional intelligence can really help you with social interaction in so many ways. These were only three examples – there are so many more ways that it can help you. So, this is just another reason to learn how to develop your emotional intelligence.

Conclusion

Now you have learned all about emotional intelligence and social skills, emotional intelligence and relationships, how to apply emotional intelligence, and of course, most importantly, how to develop it. Since you have learned all of this, the next step is to start putting it into practice in your everyday life. Emotional intelligence can help you greatly in so many situations. No matter how hard a situation may seem, with emotional intelligence it will be easier to get through. Take what you have learned from this book and use it to start living a better life today. It is not hard, and it will definitely be very rewarding!

Thank you and good luck!